Original title:
Citrus Serenade

Copyright © 2025 Creative Arts Management OÜ
All rights reserved.

Author: Lorenzo Barrett
ISBN HARDBACK: 978-1-80566-669-1
ISBN PAPERBACK: 978-1-80566-954-8

Garden Serenade for the Senses

In a grove where the lemons play,
They dance with the oranges all day.
A grapefruit giggles in the sun,
Singing songs of zesty fun.

Limes roll on a citrus spree,
Winking at bees, so cheeky and free.
With each twist, a fragrant surprise,
Tickling noses, oh what a guise!

Tangerines join in with a cheer,
Swirling their peels, oh so dear.
A slice of laughter, bright and round,
Bouncing joyfully off the ground.

In this garden, a zestful play,
Flavorful mischief in every sway.
Come join the fun, let's take a whirl,
Where fruit is dancing, and laughter swirls!

Wistful Whiffs of Fruitful Memories

In a grove where lemons dance,
Limes giggle in their vibrant pants.
Oranges roll with zest so grand,
While grapefruits play in silly bands.

The trees wear smiles, oh what a sight,
As fruit fairies twirl in pure delight.
A tangerine whispers, 'Catch my breath!'
And makes the squirrels laugh till death.

The Bright Tones of Citrus Constellations

Stars align in citrus hues,
With tangy tales and fruity clues.
Mandarins launch into the sky,
While clementines giggle and fly.

Juicy planets spin round and round,
In this orchard, joy is found.
Kumquats chime with laughter bright,
As shooting stars bring dreams to light.

Sunshine and Harmony in Bloom

Sunshine drips from every leaf,
A playful twist of sweet belief.
Bananas strut with silly glee,
While passionfruit sings off-key.

Bees buzz around in fruity cheer,
Mixing nectar with juicy beer.
Lemonade rainbows fill the air,
With flavors bold, nothing can compare.

The Palette of Nature's Juiciness

Colors splash on orchard walls,
With laughter bouncing in the halls.
Grapes tumble in a skipping race,
Chasing berries with playful grace.

Peaches wink and tease the light,
While cherries dance, a joyful sight.
In this canvas, bright and spry,
Where fruits and laughter dance and fly.

The Taste of Summer's Secrets

Lemons whisper jokes from trees,
As oranges giggle in the breeze.
Limes add a twist, a cheeky grin,
While grapefruits sing—a fruit parade to win.

The sun begins its warming tease,
Citrus dances, bringing ease.
A lemonade stand on the street,
With slippery slips and sticky feet.

Verdant Valleys and Sweet Delights

In valleys lush with green and gold,
Fruits hang low, adventures bold.
Tangerines tumble, causing a ruck,
While pomelos prank—oh what luck!

With every bite, a laugh erupts,
As juicy bits form citrus cups.
Bananas slip with a playful shout,
In this sweet world, there's never doubt.

Shades of Passionate Fruit

Passion fruit blushes, oh so shy,
Kiwis bounce with a joyful cry.
Grapes giggle in purple rows,
As nectarines burst with sunlit shows.

Mangoes flirt with every peel,
A juicy drop—what a deal!
Orchards chuckle, laughter spills,
Fruity follies, the heart it thrills.

Sun Drizzled Moments of Delight

Sunny days bring zestful cheer,
Every fruit whispers, "Come near!"
Pineapples dance with hula flair,
While cherries chuckle without a care.

In bowls of sorbet, laughter swirls,
As fruity flavors do their twirls.
Citrus fun under skies so bright,
Making memories, pure delight.

Slices of Sun-Kissed Bliss

Peeling laughter from a zest,
Orange giggles in a fest.
Lemons leap, a pucker play,
Grapefruits dance, hip-hip-hooray!

In the sun, they jump and twirl,
Roll away, a citrus swirl.
Lime's jokes, oh, what a hit,
Silly smiles, they never quit!

Melodies of Lemon and Lime

Lime serenades, a twisty tune,
Lemon laughs beneath the moon.
With each note, they sing and spin,
Drops of zest, let the fun begin!

Grapes roll by with cheeky strut,
While oranges giggle, "What's the fuss?"
Tart and sweet, a fruity rhyme,
Together they dance, it's citrus time!

Sunlit Grove Reverie

In a grove where citrus sighs,
Lemon trees wear fruit-filled ties.
Lime bushes make a joke or two,
Even oranges join the crew!

Branches tickle, laughter flows,
Sunbeams dance on peels that glow.
Bumblebees buzz with delight,
In this grove, all is just right!

Citrus Dreams in the Orchard

In dreams where tangerines prance,
Lemons waltz in a funny dance.
Oranges chuckle, ripe and round,
In this orchard, joy is found!

When grapefruits tell a pun or two,
The trees all giggle, "Who knew?"
Fragrant breezes lift the cheer,
In this land, the fun is clear!

The Glow of Garden Harvests

In gardens bright, the fruits do sing,
Lemons dance, and oranges swing.
A tangerine slips on its peel,
While grapefruits giggle, oh what a meal!

Come pluck the fruits of summer's glee,
But watch your steps, there's a bumblebee!
With squishy plums and juicy treats,
The harvest's joy is none but sweet.

Lush Labyrinth of Fruit Fantasia

In a maze of trees where colors burst,
Mango mischief went unrehearsed.
A pear with pride, a kiwi so spry,
They've conspired to make fruit pie!

Banana clowning, trying to climb,
Says he's ripe but thinks it's time.
With every twist and playful turn,
The fruity friends together yearn.

The Zesty Cadence of Nature's Songs

Lime lost his keys, while dancing around,
To the citrus beat, such a silly sound!
A smooth-skinned orange joined in the beat,
As each zesty note made them feel sweet!

Mirthful lemons, quick with a joke,
Told a lime that he was just "so broke".
A chorus of laughter from the tree,
Nature's orchestra, wild and free.

Sipping Sunshine in a Glass Jar

In a jar of glass, sunshine we sip,
Every drop tastes like a sweet trip.
The straws are dancing, doing the twist,
As the lemonade starts to mist!

Grapefruit floats like a surfer's dream,
Catch the waves of citrus cream.
With every slurp, the fun's alive,
It's a party in a jar, let's all thrive!

The Dance of Zesty Colors

Lemons twirl in vibrant cheer,
Limes giggle, oh so near,
Oranges roll and take the stage,
Grapefruits flip with all their rage.

Mangoes join with silly glee,
Bananas dance so whimsically,
In this fruit parade, they prance,
Under sunlight, they all dance.

Bright Bursts of Shimmering Light

Tangerines glow with a wink,
Like little suns, they make us think,
Each slice reveals a burst of cheer,
As laughter bounces, oh so near.

Pineapples wear their hats so bright,
Radiating joy, a funny sight,
Together, they play hide and seek,
In a fruity game, so unique.

Whirls of Juicy Emotions

Melons spin in silly glee,
Like dancers at a vibrant spree,
Berries throw their hats in the air,
As laughter fills the fragrant fair.

Grapes tumble down with a squeal,
In this zany, zest-filled reel,
Cherries laugh, their cheeks so red,
In this silly fruit fest, we're led.

The Aroma of Orange Days

Lift your nose to the bright skies,
Where citrus jokes and laughter flies,
Scented breezes bring the smiles,
As fruits play in comedic styles.

Lemonade spills with vibrant grace,
Citrus chuckles all over the place,
In this fragrant, funny craze,
We dance through our orange days.

The Zesty Heartbeat of Nature

In the grove where lemons smile,
Limes giggle with a cheeky style.
Oranges dance in the warm breeze,
Bananas sneak in with such ease.

Grapefruits toss their hats on high,
While tangerines fly by, oh my!
Nature's orchestra plays so bright,
With fruity pranks, what a delight!

Swinging branches, a citrus cheer,
Even apples roll with a snear.
The roots rumble in playful glee,
In this zesty jubilee!

Vibrant colors, bold and loud,
Citron's call brings in the crowd.
A juicy rhythm, all unwind,
In this heart that's zesty defined.

Juicy Echoes of the Cosmos

Stars twinkle like a tart delight,
Comets zoom past with zestful flight.
Planets spin on a citrus rack,
In fruity whispers, they won't hold back.

Neptune's blue like a fresh spritz,
Mars' red—oh, what a tart blitz!
Galaxies swirl in a tangy spin,
From cosmic kitchens, fun begins!

Saturn's rings made of lime zest,
Jupiter bounces—oh, what a jest!
In the universe's juicy game,
Echoes of laughter—never the same.

Celestial fruits, high above,
Making light of the stars we love.
In the vastness, we celebrate,
Juicy wonders that resonate.

Harvest Song of Tangy Delight

With baskets full of limes and zest,
The harvest dance, it's simply the best.
We twirl and skip through fields so green,
Each fruit a joke, a merry scene.

The apples giggle as they drop,
While peaches bounce and never stop.
Berries toss their hats in cheer,
Echoing joy for all to hear.

Oh, the fragrance fills the air,
As grapefruits swing without a care.
We sing our song, all full of mirth,
Celebrating this fruity birth.

There's mischief in every bite,
A playful tease, oh such delight!
In every harvest, laughter flows,
In our tangy tale, joy grows.

Fragrant Spheres Under the Sun

Lemons roll down a sunny hill,
Chasing each other for a thrill.
The sun smiles brightly, casting rays,
On this fruity fun, we all sway.

Melons laugh and splash about,
In a playful game, there's no doubt.
Juicy laughter fills the air,
A citrus world beyond compare.

Orange slices, stacked so high,
Juggling dreams under the sky.
With every wink, a zestful cheer,
Beneath the sun, we have no fear.

In fragrant spheres, the fun's begun,
A tangy race, we all run.
With nature's humor, life's a pun,
In this world of joy, we won!

A Symphony of Citrus Notes

Juicy jests on trees so bright,
Lemon jokes in morning light.
Tangerines in a merry dance,
Grapefruit giggles, take a chance.

Tickling taste buds, oh what fun,
Oranges chuckle, one by one.
In every slice, a laughter peeks,
Fragrant whispers, fruity tweaks.

Sweetness in the Segment

Each slice bursts with silly glee,
Fruit-filled laughter, come see me!
Tart and sweet, they tease and play,
Witty wedges brighten the day.

Puns on peels, a citrus show,
Jokes that only oranges know.
Limes roll in with sly delight,
Lemon wit shines bright and bright.

The Limoncello Lullaby

Sipping light in a sunny glow,
Lemon songs begin to flow.
Each note tangy, a cheeky chime,
A tune that's perfect every time.

Dancing cups on a breezy night,
Limoncello takes its flight.
With every sip, a giggle slips,
A zesty rhythm, fun-filled trips.

Orange Blossoms and Afternoon Light

In gardens where the blossoms sway,
Oranges laugh and softly play.
Petals flutter, a funny sight,
Beneath the warm and golden light.

Whispers dance on the gentle breeze,
Ticklish thoughts among the trees.
With every breeze, a comic cheer,
Sweetness blooms, the joy is here.

Autumn's Touch on Citrus Beauty

Leaves are falling, kids are laughing,
Squirrel with orange slices, snacking.
Sunshine hopping, bright and breezy,
Lemons in the wind, feeling cheesy.

Pumpkins rolling, in a race,
Tangerines join with happy face.
Citrus laughter fills the air,
Juggling oranges without a care.

Tart and sweet, a playful game,
Tossing fruit, no one's to blame.
The harvest dance, a merry spree,
In this orchard, wild and free.

So gather 'round, let's have a cheer,
For autumn's gifts and zesty beer.
With every bite, a giggle grows,
A funny tale that nature shows.

The Burst of Flavorful Mornings

Morning sun, the zest awakens,
Juicy oranges, dreams are shaken.
Coffee brews, a citrus twist,
Sips with giggles, can't resist.

Bright fruits bouncing on the table,
Who knew breakfast could be fable?
Lemonade dreams in glasses tall,
Sipping slowly, we won't fall.

Pancakes topped with grapefruit finery,
Dancing flavors, oh so shiny.
Whipped cream clouds, a playful swirl,
Tasting laughter, watch it twirl!

A fruit parade, let's start the day,
Orange confetti, hip-hip-hooray!
Bursting flavors, never whiny,
Mornings sweet and oh-so-fine-y.

Orchard Chimes in the Breeze

Swings are creaking, branches sway,
Limes are singing in the fray.
Whistle tunes with twirling kin,
Frolic here, let joy begin.

Chimes of citrus, laughter races,
Lemons dancing in their places.
Kites are flying, oh so high,
Citrus giggles fill the sky.

Squirrels juggling, nuts galore,
Oranges rolling on the floor.
Every fruit has found its sound,
In this orchard, joy is found.

Let's shout out, sing like crazy,
Grapefruits laughing, feeling hazy.
In the breeze, we'll find our flair,
Orchard chimes, without a care.

A Melody of Zesty Sunshine

Sunshine strumming on a lute,
Tropical tunes, a fruity hoot.
Dance with limes, a merry beat,
Zesty rhythms, can't be beat.

Bouncing lemons in the sun,
Skipping songs, oh what fun!
Tango with the vibrant fruits,
Salsa moves in polka boots.

Mangoes twirl, papayas sway,
Sing along, it's a fruit buffet!
With every bite, a silly sound,
Zingy laughter all around.

As the day melts into night,
Citrus dreams take happy flight.
In this melody of delight,
Zesty sunshine, pure and bright.

Golden Orbs of Summer

Golden orbs hang high with glee,
Lemons giggle, oh so free.
Limes roll sideways, what a sight,
Dancing shadows in soft light.

Sour faces make us laugh,
Juice spills out, a citrus bath.
Fruits in hats, a comical scene,
Sunshine splashes, bright and keen.

Pineapples wear their spiky crowns,
Oranges chase their silly clowns.
Grapefruits bounce in playful cheer,
Summer's joy is finally here!

With every slice, a chuckle grows,
Jokes served up where laughter flows.
These golden orbs from tree to stand,
Bring a smile across the land.

Zestful Whispers in the Breeze

Lemons whisper secrets sweet,
Spinning tales of summer heat.
Grapefruit giggles as it flips,
Limes tell jokes with zesty quips.

A breeze rushes, tickling skin,
Citrus pranks begin to spin.
Bananas slip with giddy grace,
While oranges roll, a silly race.

Lime light shines on melting ice,
Fruit salad talks, oh so nice.
Suspense builds, two halves collide,
Juicy laughter won't subside.

Under sunlit skies we play,
In a zesty, chipper way.
Fruitful friendships take their chance,
In the breeze, we waltz and dance.

Sunlit Juice of Joy

A splash of sunlight, bright and bold,
Oranges laugh, their stories told.
With every squeeze, a chuckle flows,
Sippin' sunshine, joy bestows.

Lemonade stands become a stage,
For fruity jokes, we all engage.
Underneath this vibrant hue,
Watermelons sing, just for you.

Fruits parade in rows so neat,
Lemons in tuxes, quite the treat!
A kiwi juggles, what a sight,
As cherries giggle, day and night.

Glasses clink, the fun won't stop,
With every drop, we rise and bop.
Sunlit juice, a playful spree,
Laughter bubbling, wild and free.

The Tangy Dance of Fruit

Tangerines twirl in a round,
As berries bounce upon the ground.
Citrusy rhythms in the air,
A fruity dance, beyond compare.

Bananas slip with curious grace,
While apples join the lively chase.
Dancing lemons, zest on fire,
Swaying high, they'll never tire.

Grapefruits glide, their pinks so bright,
In a fruity frenzy, pure delight.
With every shake, a chuckle grows,
As citrus surprises steal the shows.

A kilted lime and a polka-dot peel,
Bring smiles and laughter that we can feel.
In this tangy dance, we find our groove,
Fruits unite, let's all approve!

Sun-soaked Spirit of Citrus

Under sunlit skies, the fruits take a stand,
Lemonade rivers, oh how they expand!
Grapefruits are giggling, oranges conspire,
In this zesty fiesta, we all dare to aspire.

Limes roll on the floor, trying hard to dance,
While tangerines chuckle, not missing their chance.
A citrus parade, with peels in the air,
Laughter erupts; it's a juicy affair.

The lemonade fountain, a slippery ride,
Sipping sweet nectar, we laugh at the tide.
With each splash of fun, we slip and we slide,
In this citrus wonder, who needs to abide?

So raise up your glasses, toast to the day,
With zest and with cheer, come what may!
In this sun-soaked spirit, let laughter ignite,
As we bite into joy, and find sheer delight!

The Harvest of Bright Delights

In gardens of yellow, where fruit bursts with cheer,
A bounty of laughter, the harvest draws near.
With baskets of joy, we gather the fun,
Each orange a giggle, each lemon a pun.

Grapefruits gossip, sharing secrets so bright,
They whisper of flavor that tickles the night.
With laughter in the air, we peel back the rhyme,
No better exhilaration than citrus at prime!

Marmalade mischief becomes our delight,
We spread it on toast, a sweet morning bite.
As fruit confesses, with giggles galore,
Each slice is a story we simply adore.

So dance with the zest, let the humor unfold,
In this ripe celebration, be daring, be bold!
Enthralled by these treasures, we're all feeling light,
In the harvest of giggles, the world feels just right!

Sweets of Nature's Serenade

In fields of bright colors, the laughter is sweet,
Fruits singing tunes with every small treat.
Lemon pies parade, all frosted with cheer,
While orange-flavored giggles ring out loud and clear.

Citron confetti twirls up to the sky,
Bananas are laughing, oh my, oh my!
With peels for confetti, we celebrate bliss,
In this carnival of flavors, you won't want to miss.

Sipping on nectar, we dance through the day,
Each drop of joy brightens our playful way.
With berries around us, we skip and we twirl,
In this nature's sweet symphony, watch the fun unfurl!

So relish the laughter, let sweetness abound,
As nature's own treasures bring joy all around.
Let's bathe in the giggles, soak up the sun,
This spirited romp, oh, it's just so much fun!

Lively Limes and Vibrant Vistas

Oh lively limes, in a row, what a sight!
With zest and with tang, they party all night.
In the sun's glow, they roll and they rhyme,
Each twist of their peel is a jester's good time.

Vistas of vibrance stretch far and wide,
As lemons dance lightly, they take us for a ride.
With juice-flavored jokes that tickle and tease,
Their humor's contagious; it brings us to our knees!

Tasting the citrus, a zing in the air,
We'll giggle and wiggle, forgetting our care.
With slices so bright, a burst of delight,
Lively limes lead us into the night.

So let us be merry, let laughter resound,
With vibrant sun-soaked flavors all around.
In this fresh, funny world, we embrace what we find,
As limes and their laughter intertwine joyfully aligned!

Citrus Kaleidoscope of Dreams

In a swirl of orange and lime,
Silly thoughts dance in rhyme.
Lemons giggle in the sun,
While grapefruits just want to run.

Tangerines in a quirky hat,
Chasing after a playful cat.
Pineapple swings on a vine,
Sipping juice, feeling fine!

Juggling fruit with a grin,
Tumbling and tumbling, it's a win.
Limes jump over a rainbow,
With laughter that steals the show!

As night falls, they play charades,
Orange puns in sweet cascades.
In this fruity, wild delight,
Every moment shines so bright!

Dancing on a Citrus Wave

Surfing on a lemon zest,
Twirling and spinning, feel the best.
Oranges cheer from the shore,
While grapefruits shout for more!

Limes rock with a funky beat,
Pumping rhythm in the street.
A peach joins in with a wave,
As all the fruit hearts rave.

Bounce with plums beneath the sun,
Swaying, spinning—oh what fun!
Banana splits the spotlight bright,
As all join in for a dance tonight!

The tidal wave of juice flows free,
Sticky feet from the jubilee.
With every laugh and every grin,
This fruity party shall begin!

The Character of Orchard Magic

In a grove where laughter grows,
An apple tells a joke, who knows?
While pears giggle in delight,
Plums roll over, what a sight!

A zesty orange wears a crown,
Declaring, "Let's not frown!"
Bananas slip and slide on grass,
In a race that's sure to pass!

A bushy sage with sage advice,
Says "Taste this drink, it's really nice!"
Grapes whisper secrets under shade,
In this orchard, fun is made!

Cherries burst with laughter loud,
Creating a joyful crowd.
With each moment, magic brews,
In the orchard, there's no blues!

Pondering Under Lemon-Laden Trees

Underneath the yellow glow,
Lemons ponder, tales in tow.
"Why do we roll?" a lime does ask,
"Oranges just bask in a mask!"

Lemonade dreams fill the air,
With giggles laden everywhere.
A grapefruit sighs, "Life's a squeeze,"
Finding joy in simple tease.

The trees giggle with their fruit,
Debating who is cuter, who's astute.
Under this zesty, sun-kissed dome,
Every fruit finds a home!

Pondering sweet life's fruit parade,
In citrus worlds, fun is made.
With chuckles sprouting like bright blooms,
Under trees, laughter resumes!

The Orchard's Melodic Breeze

In the grove where oranges dance,
Lemons giggle, given the chance.
Limes roll over, all in a spin,
While grapefruits sing, let the fun begin!

A tangerine in a silly hat,
Claims he's the king, imagine that!
Pears start twirling, join the cheer,
While cherries just burst out in a sneer.

Peaches joke, 'Make way for me!
I'm the juiciest fruit, can't you see?'
But apples quip, 'Hold your applause!
We've got the crunch; that's just the laws!'

The breeze carries laughter, oh what a sight,
As fruits on branches dance day and night.
Nature's chorus, merry and bright,
In this fruity fiesta, pure delight!

Sunkissed Moments on a Canvas

Under a sun that paints the day,
Citrusy jesters swing and sway.
Grapefruits pull a funny face,
While lemons juggle in a race!

A lime says, 'I'm zesty and light!',
But a banana slips, oh what a fright!
Tangerines giggle, rolling so round,
While in the grass, kumquats abound.

Paint the sky with colors so bold,
As fruits laugh together, tales to be told.
Orange and yellow, a canvas of cheer,
Each stroke of humor draws friends near.

In the gallery of nature's delight,
Every fruit shows off its best light.
With sunshine as the artist's hand,
Together in jest, they make a stand!

Fruitful Harmonies at Dusk

Evening falls; the orchard hums,
A chorus where the laughter comes.
Grapes tumble down in giggling rolls,
While apples boast of their shiny souls.

A tangerine sings with a voice so sweet,
While lemons tap dance with zesty feet.
Peaches sway, brushing the night,
Bouncing around, oh what a sight!

In the twilight glow, cherries tease,
'Catch us, catch us!' on a gentle breeze.
As limes do cartwheels, plucky in jest,
Every fruit wants to showcase their best.

Together they blend in nature's song,
A symphony of humor, where all belong.
As daylight fades and night falls clear,
The orchard hums sweet tunes, full of cheer!

Radiant Slices of Sweetness

Morning breaks with a laughter spree,
Where slices of joy hang from each tree.
A grapefruit says, 'I'm the sweetest slice!'
While a lemon adds, 'I'm tangy and nice!'

Orange wedges laugh with delight,
As they peel away, oh what a sight!
Bananas crake jokes with a curious peel,
'What do you call fruit that can't keep it real?'

They dangle and sway in the vibrant sun,
Sharing their stories, just having fun.
Kumquats giggling, sticking together,
Finding sweet solace in sunny weather.

Radiant fruit under skies so blue,
Each slice a friend, honest and true.
In this fruity world where laughter's the key,
They sing of sweetness, wild and free!

The Symphony of Citrus Days

In gardens bright, the lemons dance,
With every twist, they take a chance.
Limes giggle as they roll away,
Twirling zestfully in bright array.

Oranges sing a cheery tune,
While grapefruits bask beneath the moon.
A pickle joins in, much to dismay,
Saying, 'Hey! I'm here to play!'

Marmalade dreams and jelly fights,
Sugary laughter fills the nights.
With citrus cheer, we raise our cups,
Toast to the fruit that lifts us up!

So gather 'round for juiciness,
In fruity fun we'll find our bliss.
With every squirt, life's tastes are found,
In this zesty land, we spin around!

Sunlit Gardens and Juicy Tales

In gardens lush, the oranges grin,
As butterflies take flight and spin.
Lemonade rivers flow with glee,
Splashes of joy for you and me.

Tales of grapefruits, sour and sweet,
Dance in the breeze with a citrus beat.
The limes hold court, they reign so bold,
With zestful stories waiting to be told.

Kids make crowns of clementines,
Wearing them proudly, loving the signs.
In this sunlit place, laughter sails,
Echoing bright in juicy tales.

So gather 'round, let's share a slice,
Of citrus dreams that taste so nice.
With every giggle and funny rhyme,
We'll squeeze the joy and share the time!

Squeeze of Life's Sweetness

In life's bright kitchen, fruit's in line,
A citrus squeeze, a glass of sunshine.
Grapefruits burst with laughter loud,
While lemons smirk and feign so proud.

Orange peels fly like chuckles bright,
Zesty giggles fill the night.
Limes play pranks with cheeky flair,
Rolling away, they're quite the pair.

A smoothie party's just begun,
With citrus fruits, we'll have some fun.
Straws like swords, let's take a fight,
In this sweetness, everything's all right.

So when life serves a tangy twist,
Just squeeze the joy; you can't resist.
Through every hug and citrus cheer,
We'll sip the sweetness, have no fear!

Tangerine Skies at Twilight

As daylight dims, tangerines glow,
Under the sky, they steal the show.
With every slice, a laugh does fly,
In twilight's glow, our spirits high.

Kumquats chime in, a quirky band,
Playing tunes, oh so unplanned.
While oranges tell jokes about fate,
'Why did the lemon feel so great?'

With laughter rippling through the air,
Lemon drops fall without a care.
Each citrus smile is a funny tease,
As starlight twinkles, bringing ease.

So let's embrace this twilight thrill,
With fruity puns and hearts to fill.
Beneath tangerine skies, we'll gleefully sway,
In this citrus realm, where joy will play!

Citrus Ripples in Time

In an orchard where laughs collide,
Lemons dance, no need to hide.
Oranges chuckle under the sun,
Jokes between peels, oh what fun!

A grapefruit juggles with some zest,
While limes attempt a juggling quest.
Chortles echo in every tree,
As fruits wrestle with glee and glee!

With each bite, a giggle grows,
Pulp-friends sharing silly shows.
Bouncing balls of tangy cheer,
Time flies fast, the fun is near!

So grab a slice, enjoy the ride,
In this fruity world, joy won't hide.
With every squeeze, a joke is brewed,
Life's a laugh when you're citrus-stewed!

An Ode to Fruity Delights

In a bowl of colors bright,
Fruits gather, oh what a sight!
They giggle as they start to play,
Bananas lead the dance today.

Apples chase, with a wink and sigh,
While cherries tumble, oh my, oh my!
Pineapples wear hats, sharp and grand,
Melons roll like they're in a band.

With fruity laughter, they unite,
Creating joy from morning light.
Silly sounds as they all collide,
In this fruity fun, we take pride!

So raise a toast to each delight,
For laughter finds a way, all right.
With every slice, a giggle leaps,
And in our hearts, the joy still keeps!

Golden Orbs of Joy

Golden orbs swing from their stems,
Fruits unite in cheeky gems.
Lemons laugh, their zest on fire,
While tangerines join the choir.

Limes tell tales, with spritz and cheer,
Of fruity capers throughout the year.
Grapes join in with a bunch of pranks,
Tickling the juice with their merry flanks.

As they roll down the orchard floor,
Each fruity joke opens a door.
To laughter's realm, where all is bright,
Golden orbs shine day and night.

So gather 'round, come share the glee,
In this orchard, we're fruity and free.
With every bite, the fun won't cease,
Golden moments that never lease!

Zestful Whispers in the Breeze

In the meadow where aromas twine,
Fruits converse, oh so divine!
Lime whispers secrets, oh so sly,
While oranges giggle, passing by.

With every breeze, a chuckle grows,
As apple pies share their prose.
Pears spread tales of mischief sweet,
While berries dance on little feet.

Grapefruit winks from a sunny mound,
Dancing to the zesty sound.
Sours and sweets in joyful spree,
Creating laughter, wild and free.

So join the fun, let giggles rise,
Underneath these juicy skies.
A world where fruits bring pure delight,
Making every day feel bright!

Citrus Clouds and Skyward Dreams

Lemon drops falling from a tree,
Orange giggles bounce with glee.
Lime slices dance in the bright sun,
Peel back the laughter, oh what fun!

Grapefruit hats on heads so round,
Juicy jokes spill onto the ground.
Tangerine tails wagging in air,
Sour faces turn into flair!

Mango mirth in a zesty breeze,
A fruity parade that's sure to please.
Tart little berries join the line,
Together they frolic, so divine!

With citrus clouds so fluffy and high,
Citrus dreams floating, oh my, oh my!
Join the juice jive, don't miss out,
Bubbly laughs, what it's all about!

Sing to Me, O Sweetly Ripe Fruits

Oh sing to me, you juicy delights,
With melodies bright on summer nights.
Harmonies wrapped in peels so bright,
Fruits that make my heart take flight.

Lemon can croon in zesty tones,
While orange laughs and shakes its bones.
Berry choruses tangle and twist,
In this fruity concert, not to be missed!

Mangoes wail in a tropical tune,
With laughter that dances like a balloon.
Papayas pluck strings that sparkle and shine,
Each bite a note, a taste divine!

So gather round, my friends, let's sing,
To the fruits of summer, let joy take wing.
With every harmony, our spirits climb,
In this fruity opera, we're all in our prime!

Summer's Jive Wrapped in Rind

Wobble and wiggle, the melon prances,
As sunlight glistens, the fruit advances.
Peaches sway with a jolly grin,
In this summer jive, everybody wins!

Citrus twirls in a playful spree,
With zestful dances that set us free.
Lemons laugh as they spin and roll,
Join the fruit fiesta, let's all lose control!

Lime kicks high, orange struts tall,
Each fruity groove makes a party call.
With juice-filled laughter, we shout hooray,
In the summer ballet, we waft and sway!

So grab a slice, take your place,
In this vibrant dance of fruity grace.
With every bite, joy takes the lead,
Our hearts are full, our souls are freed!

The Balm of Citrus Notes

In the garden of tangy delight,
Where sunshine gleams, everything's bright.
Grapefruits giggle, drenching us sweet,
A balm for the soul, a zesty treat!

With a wink, lime brings a tangy song,
While oranges cheer, they all sing along.
Lemonade laughter floods the day,
With citrus notes to keep blues at bay!

Melons jive with a juicy rush,
While kiwi dreams turn into a hush.
Each slice a melody, crisp and clear,
Turning sad frowns into smiles and cheer!

So gather the fruits, let joy ignite,
In this citrus balm, everything feels right.
With every sip, let the laughter flow,
In this world of laughter, let's steal the show!

The Depiction of Tangy Memories

In a jar of sunshine, I found my glee,
Lemons giggle, oh so free.
They bounce around like little jesters,
Tickling noses, like happy testers.

Oranges wear a peely grin,
Sipping juice, I dance and spin.
Lime jumps in with zesty flair,
Citrusy humor hanging in the air.

Grapefruits frown, but oh so sweet,
Sour pouts can't hide the treat.
Each tang a laugh, a citrus joke,
A zesty punch that makes me croak.

Memories twist in a fruit-filled parade,
Juicy smiles in every shade.
With a wink and zesty cheer,
I sip the humor year by year.

Refreshing Melodies in a Glass

Lemonade whispers, summer's tune,
Sipping slow beneath the moon.
Mint leaves dance in frosty glee,
Bubbles bounce, so wild and free.

A splash of zest fills up the cup,
Like giggling friends, we lift it up.
Lime's high notes, a citrus choir,
Tickling throats like joyful fire.

Squeezed joy drips in every sip,
Strawberries join for a serenade trip.
Orange peels twirl, a dandy show,
As laughter flows, the flavors grow.

When tasted slow, the magic's swift,
In every gulp, I find a gift.
Bubbly joy in a swirling dance,
A refreshing tune, a zesty chance.

Echoes of Citrus Breezes

In the garden, scents collide,
Tangerines and giggles glide.
Lime trees sway in the playful air,
Rustling leaves with fruity flair.

Whispers tickle through the grove,
With every joke, the blossoms rove.
Lemon-laughs flutter on the breeze,
As ripe puns bloom among the trees.

Oranges bounce in a sunny loop,
While grapefruits scheme in a wobbly troop.
Each citrus jest, a lively tune,
Winking stars in the afternoon.

Echoes of zest, playful and bright,
Fill the world with pure delight.
With every giggle, a tree does sway,
Citrus magic jokes all day.

Sweetness Unleashed in Bloom

Peering close, I see them sprout,
Citrus giggles through the doubt.
Blooms of yellow, orange, and green,
Bursting joy, a playful scene.

With every squeeze, a chuckle flies,
Like playful sprites in summer skies.
Lemon drop laughs, a sweet parade,
Whisk of happiness in the shade.

In sweet delight, the blossoms play,
Twisting humor in the sun's ballet.
Grapefruit jokes whirled in the air,
A mouthful of fun beyond compare.

When harvest comes, the giggles flow,
With zest unleashed, the smiles grow.
In every bite, the sweetness gleams,
A funny world where joy redeems.

Nectarine Nocturne

Under the moon, fruit flies dance,
Nectarines waltz in a fruity romance.
With laughter and juice, they spin round,
In the orchard night, silliness found.

Peaches are giggling, lemons are sly,
Tangerines chuckle as they roll by.
The laughter bubbles in fruit-laden air,
Messy delight, without a care.

Zesty jokes shared in every bite,
Citrusy puns that feel just right.
Everyone's biting with sweet, juicy glee,
It's a fruity fiesta beneath the tree.

As the sun dips low, the fun's not done,
Who knew fruit could make you run?
With slips and slides in pulp and juice,
Orchard laughter, let's cut loose!

Sun-Drenched Citrus Wishes

A lemon slice dreams in warm sunlight,
Hoping to become a drink tonight.
With wishes whispered on golden breeze,
A citrus wish to tickle with ease.

Orange bursts with a giggly glow,
Sharing secrets that only fruits know.
"Squeeze me tight," they all chant loud,
Citrusy humor makes us proud.

Grapefruits join, brimming with cheer,
Dancing zestfully, come draw near.
With every squirt and every peel,
The laughter rises, it's a fruity deal.

In the warmth of sun, we feel so fine,
Laughter rolls on like sweet old wine.
Wishing big in this juicy universe,
Fruity dreams that never disperse.

The Bite of Juicy Moments

In a orchard full of pranks galore,
Each fruit's a joker, nothing's a bore.
A biting jest from a cheeky pear,
Laughter erupts from everywhere!

Melon rolls down, full of surprise,
Telling tales that would mesmerize.
Each juicy moment, a sweet delight,
Fruity love songs fly through the night.

Limes laugh harder, they're sour and bold,
Their zesty punch is a sight to behold.
With giggles and splashes of vibrant zest,
Each bite brings joy, it's what we do best.

So here's to the moments, juicy and bright,
Where laughter and fruit make everything right.
Join in this tale of flavor and fun,
In every bite, let liveliness run!

Orchard Reflections

In the orchard's mirror, we glance and grin,
Bananas are laughing, they're ripe for sin.
With each twist and turn on the breezy swing,
Fruits tell stories of the joy they bring.

Ripe old apples spin tales of yore,
Of pie-making nights and more, oh so lore.
Plump cherries chuckle, they know the game,
All in good fun, no one's to blame.

Beneath leafy canopies, laughter unfolds,
Tangy tales in the sun-warmed golds.
With jests and jives under bright summer skies,
Each fruit's a comedian, a fun surprise.

So let's raise a glass to the orchard's cheer,
With fruity reflections that bring us near.
Each slice, each bite, a story to share,
Join the laughter, if you dare!

Lemonade Dreams and Orange Hues

A glass of yellow smiles, oh so sweet,
Dancing flavors twirl on tiny feet.
Sips of sunshine, laughter in the air,
A splash of giggles, joy everywhere.

Pair it with a doughnut, what a treat!
Sugar-coated dreams, can't be beat.
Lemonade laughter spills from the glass,
Bring your friends and let the fun amass.

With ice cubes clinking, whispers of cheer,
Silly stories told, we disappear.
Frogs in top hats, and ducks in a line,
In our lemonade world, everything's fine.

Running through fields with zest in our veins,
Like a bubble of giggles, it remains.
Juggling lemons, or maybe just fate,
In this zesty realm, we celebrate!

The Tang of Sunshine's Embrace

Bright tangy moments, on our lips, they land,
Lemon zest giggles, drawn by the hand.
Tickle the taste buds, sunshine's delight,
A twist of laughter in the warm twilight.

Silly oranges dance, in a fruity parade,
Witty anecdotes that never do fade.
Juggling juice puns like a circus clown,
In this tangerine town, we never frown.

With swings made of grapefruit, we soar and glide,
Building dreams in baskets, nothing to hide.
Spinning in circles with juicy delight,
The tang of our laughter, forever in sight.

Sunshine on our cheeks, and sparkles in our eyes,
Orange juice kisses, beneath sunny skies.
We sip and we giggle, let the fun soar high,
In the tang of our joy, we reach for the sky!

Limoncello Lullabies Under the Moon

Sweet lemon dreams, drift on breezy nights,
Dancing in shadows, with soft glowing lights.
Sipping on laughter, as the moon peeks in,
Every giggle a magic, where do we begin?

With limoncello whispers, soft and divine,
Tickling our senses, a twist of the line.
Puns in the air like fireflies at play,
Giggling together till the break of day.

A serenade of silly, with laughter that blooms,
The stars join our party, banishing glooms.
Sip by sip, we float on a sweet melody,
In this lullaby land, we find harmony.

Moonlit mischief, each splash a delight,
Creating sweet moments, twinkling so bright.
As shadows dance lightly, our giggles will rise,
In limoncello dreams, we embrace the skies!

Nectarine Nostalgia in Bloom

Nectarine drizzles on warm summer days,
Whispers of sweetness in sun-kissed rays.
We laugh as we bite, the juice runs away,
Tasting nostalgia in such silly ways.

In orchards of humor, the fruits play a part,
Jokes bloom like flowers, warming the heart.
Playful and ripe, laughter fills the air,
With nectarine nectar, each moment we share.

Squirrels wearing hats, what a sight to behold!
Chasing their tails, as stories unfold.
Fruit flies will giggle, fluttering near,
Painting our world with joy and good cheer.

Beneath these sweet branches, we bask in delight,
Creating a world where everything's bright.
Nectarine memories that never will fade,
In this funny orchard, we're happily swayed!

Rind and Rhythm of a Summer's Day

Peeling oranges in the sun,
A laughter dance has just begun.
Squirrels eye the zestful treat,
Nature's comic, quite a feat.

Juice drips down in sticky lines,
Little hands lost in sweet designs.
We hop and skip past lemon trees,
While bees buzz tunes upon the breeze.

Limes rolling like a disco ball,
A fruity party, come one, come all!
The laughter echoes, bright and clear,
Amidst the citrus, feel the cheer!

In every bite, the sun's embrace,
A slip on peel? We'll call it grace!
With citrus smiles upon our face,
This summer day, a zestful chase!

Sweet Citrus Pizzicato

Mandarins in a playful spree,
Bouncing 'round as fast as can be,
With every giggle and every pop,
We find our rhythm, never stop.

A tangerine slips, a funny sight,
Rolling down, what a fruity flight!
Kicking back with zest on our lips,
Sipping juice in silly sips.

Lemon twirls in a fancy dress,
Waltzing 'round, oh what a mess!
Slapstick lives where the oranges sway,
In the orchestra of summer play.

With laughter ringing through the air,
Fruit confetti everywhere!
A sweet serenade takes the stage,
Leaving behind a juicy page.

Juicy Secrets Beneath the Leaves

Hidden treasures in tangled vines,
Whispers of sweetness that brightly shines.
A lemon named Larry, bold and proud,
Sharing secrets with the crowd.

Behind each leaf, a riddle lies,
Giggling fruits with playful eyes.
Juicy tales on a summer's night,
Tickling taste buds, pure delight!

The lime goes "squeeze me!"—what a joke,
While grapefruits giggle, "I'll choke!"
In this garden, laughter grows,
With every twist, a secret shows.

What's the citrus's favorite game?
Peel the fruit, it's never the same!
We romp and laugh, all day, all night,
In juicy secrets, everything's bright!

Orange Blossoms in a Gentle Breeze

In the orchard, blossoms sway,
Comical critters lead the way.
An orange tree with a bowing branch,
Shared with giggles, let's take a chance!

A breeze whispers jokes to the pears,
While oranges chuckle, full of cares.
"Catch me if you can," they tease,
Rolling forth with the greatest ease.

As bees buzz out their tiny tunes,
We dance like fruit in the afternoon.
With petals swirling overhead,
Laughter blooms where joy is spread.

Orange blossoms, a funny sight,
Dancing with the stars at night.
In this grove, where humor's found,
We wear our laughter all around!

Nectar of Life in Each Slice

In a world where fruits can talk,
Lemons joke, and grapefruits gawk.
Limes laugh loud, oranges tease,
Each slice a giggle, each zest to please.

Tangerines dance with a peppy jig,
Plumping up like a happy pig.
They share their secrets with every bite,
A feast of flavors, oh what a sight!

The tangy tales they love to tell,
Under the citrusy magic spell.
Each segment's voice, a vibrant tune,
Beneath the bright and gleeful moon.

So grab a fruit, don't think twice,
Join the laughter, enjoy the slice.
Life's a joke with every tart,
In this juicy world, we play our part.

Serene Skies and Juicy Mapping

In a sky of citrus dreams so bright,
Oranges float, what a silly sight!
Kites made of lemons drift so high,
While grapefruit clouds giggle and sigh.

Below, the earth, a tangy map,
With every twist, there's a fruity clap.
Lemons lead the way with zest,
While limes follow, in their best dress.

A parade of fruits in cheerful rows,
Bouncing along where the laughter flows.
Each step taken with a juicy cheer,
All the world's brightness is gathered here.

So journey far in this fruity land,
With citrus friends who understand.
Laugh alongside, let joy combine,
In this silly tale of zest and rhyme.

A Garden of Zesty Reflections

In a garden where laughter grows,
Every fruit a cheeky pose.
Chickens chase oranges 'round the bend,
While lemons make jokes, what a friend!

Limes climb trees, so full of glee,
Swinging wildly, oh can't you see?
Grapefruits giggle as shadows play,
Under sunbeams of bright display.

A patch of laughter, vibrant and loud,
Fruits celebrating, drawing a crowd.
They share their juice, their zest for fun,
Making merry under the sun.

So wander through this garden fine,
Where fruits and jokes intertwine.
Each zesty tale, a smile to share,
In this happy grove of fruity fare.

The Rhapsody of Rind and Realm

In a realm where rinds sing and say,
Fruits frolic in a zesty ballet.
With grapefruit flutes and lemon drums,
They create a symphony that truly hums.

Rind and realm twirl in joy so bright,
A whirling dance in the warm sunlight.
Limes leap high; it's a citrus spree,
Fruits rejoicing in wild jubilee.

Choruses of oranges ring and resonate,
While grapefruits boast, feeling great.
Their zestful tunes, a comical sight,
Echoing cheer into the night.

So join this rhapsody, don't miss out,
In the fruity laughter, let's twist and shout.
Each juicy note, a smile to declare,
In the merry world of rind and flair.

Twilight's Citrus Kiss

In twilight's glow, limes dress up,
They dance around in a bumpy cup,
Lemonade laughs, with a witty grin,
While oranges plot how to sneak in.

Grapefruits giggle, a tart little crowd,
Whispering fun in a voice, quite loud,
With each little squeeze, a joke is shared,
What's the punchline? They're never scared!

Under the stars, a zesty hum,
Inventing new drinks, what could come?
From a citrus tree with fruit so bright,
Who knew they'd become the life of the night!

As crickets chirp, and peels go flying,
Lemons, you see, are always trying,
In this bold play, a blend so grand,
A twilight kiss, where flavors stand.

The Secret Life of Mandarins

In the orchard shade, they gather 'round,
Mandarins plot, their laughter abound,
With mischievous smiles, they peel away,
Jokes on the tangy side, come what may.

They wear their zesty jackets tight,
Ready for antics by day and by night,
Rolling down hills, they make such a scene,
Orange peels flying, like laughter unseen.

A tango of sweetness, so full of cheer,
The world not knowing what they hold dear,
"Life's too short," says one with a pout,
"Let's create some juice and squeeze all the doubt!"

In the orchard's heart, their secrets unfurl,
Hidden adventures in citrusy whirl,
While the humans just sip from their glass,
The mandarin crew will forever have sass!

Sweet Citrus Ballad

Oh, sweet little orange, you're quite the tease,
You roll off the table with such graceful ease,
Lemon's proud cousin, with zest on his face,
Whispering secrets in a sweet, tangy place.

A grapefruit winks with a playful twang,
"I'm bitter," he says, while the others all sang,
Now lime comes in, with a quirky dance move,
"Let's see who's got the best citrus groove!"

Together they form a colorful crew,
Making sweet tunes that are juicy and new,
With every squeeze, a laugh fills the air,
A ballad of flavors, beyond compare.

"Oh, the fun we create, with each sunny day,"
They twirl and resist being eaten away,
In their citrus world, joy multiplies fast,
In their zesty ballad, they'll forever last.

Sunset Over Citrus Fields

Beneath the sunset, the fruits have a plan,
With oranges marching, led by a fan,
They paint the sky with hues vibrant and bold,
As laughter erupts, their stories unfold.

Lemonade sips on a warm evening breeze,
Telling tall tales that are sure to please,
As grapefruits chime in with jests of delight,
Under the glow, all wrongs seem right.

From the fields they come, a zesty parade,
Kumquats in hats, each joke they've displayed,
Lime joins the fun, with a squeeze on the side,
In the twilight glow, they all take pride.

As stars appear, they dance and they sway,
In the sunset's warmth, they throw cares away,
A citrusy field where the laughter survives,
Under the moon, their spirit derives.

The Squeeze of Radiance

In a kitchen bright, with fruit piled high,
Lemons play catch, oh my, oh my!
They roll and they tumble, a zesty crew,
Squeezing out giggles, like fresh morning dew.

Oranges compete, what a juicy race,
Flinging their segments all over the place!
With laughter and juice, the fun never ends,
A fruity parade where everyone blends.

Limes join the bash, in a bitter disguise,
With jokes that go sour, quite the surprise!
They pucker and grin, the crowd's in a spin,
A zesty explosion, let the fun begin!

So raise up your glasses, with zest we toast,
To the fruit of our laughter, we all love the most!
A squeeze of delight, in every round,
Cheers to the joy in this fruity playground!

Rhapsody of Rind and Pith

In the garden's heart, where oranges sing,
Dancing and twirling, oh what a thing!
Peeling their skins, they burst into song,
A rhythm of citrus, where we all belong.

Grapefruits gossip in shades of pink,
Creating zesty tales that make us think!
With a wink and a twist, they splash us with cheer,
In this merry chorus, the end is not near.

Nectarines join with a wink and a nod,
In this playful patch, where we all applaud!
Sweetness and tang mix, a spritely refrain,
Each bite a giggle, like laughter in rain.

So gather around, let the laughter unfurl,
With pithy delights, let's dance and twirl!
For in the rhythm of fruits and sweet zest,
We find all our joy, in this playful fest!

Zephyr's Citrus Caress

A breeze brings whispers from the orchard near,
Lemons are joking, spreading good cheer!
Bouncing on branches, like kids with glee,
Swaying and laughing, wild and free.

Grapes rolling down, a slippery spree,
"Mischief is afoot!" shouts a cheeky pea!
Juicy orange jesters juggling with flair,
They toss their own segments high in the air.

With a log pile of limes, they question their fate,
"Are we sour or sweet?" they giggle and wait.
Pithy punchlines land with a squishy delight,
As the sun sets softly, bringing stars bright.

So let's ride the whirlwind of zest and delight,
With laughter as vibrant as the warmth of the night!
In this funny caper, we find our release,
In zephyr's embrace, our hearts find their peace!

Chasing Tangerine Skies

Up in the air, tangerines take flight,
Chasing the clouds, oh what a sight!
With a whimsical bounce, they soar through the blue,
Leaving trails of giggles, just passing through.

In this fruit-filled circus, all flavors collide,
Lemons leap high with a zesty glide!
Bouncing off raindrops, they laugh with delight,
As oranges splash color on the day's light.

Lost in the fun, grapefruits make a splash,
Juggling with joy, it's a zesty bash!
With peels like confetti, they dance and they spin,
In this tangy tempest, let the laughter begin!

So come join the chase, in skies bright and clear,
With flavors that tickle, and bring us near!
In this citrusy dream, we'll dive and we'll soar,
For the best kind of fun is always in store!

www.ingramcontent.com/pod-product-compliance
Lightning Source LLC
Chambersburg PA
CBHW071847160426
43209CB00003B/451